BUILD YOUR BRAND, NOT YOUR BUSINESS

EVOKING THE RIGHT EMOTIONS IN AUDIENCE PERCEPTION

Sam Skinner

Table of Contents

Chapter one

Introduction

In its earlier forms, branding was only used to denote ownership and dates all the way back to roughly 2000BC. To distinguish their cattle from other animals, farmers would brand them, and artisans would emblazon emblems on their creations to indicate where they came from. The industrial revolution and the mass market updated the usage of trademarks in the nineteenth century, causing a change. The art of branding has evolved through time; nowadays, businesses engage brand specialists and other types of professionals to develop a brand identity that distinguishes them from the competition and communicates the values and beliefs of the company. Brand identity refers to the distinguishing characteristic s of a brand in the eyes of customers, such as its color, design, and logo. To make the brand alive and elicit the desired emotions in the target audience, a brand identity system must provide the user with an experience in addition to focusing on the visual features of the brand. All start-ups need a well considered brand identity in order to be competitive on the market. In Sweden, there were 73 687 new businesses as of 2020. According to statistics, 70% of these businesses fail during the first five years. Lack of effective branding and a lack of a distinct specialty, as well as not being distinctive enough, are the top two reasons why start-up businesses fail. In a competitive market, a powerful brand stands out, and a brand's market success is directly influenced by how that brand is viewed.

1.1 Purpose

The first goal of this thesis is to provide a conceptual framework that explains how a new business should approach the process of developing a brand; the second goal is to use the framework to create a brand identity for a startup company: Thirdly,

integrate the brand
identity into the website of the business and check to see whether the intended audience connects with the identity.

1.2 Research problem
• What is a brand?
• How can a startup business build a brand that resonates with its audience?

• How can consumers be used to test a new brand?

Background (1.3)
The startup firm is developing a new software service, but they don't know how to create a brand identity that captures their vision, appeals to customers, and sets them apart from rivals. The

business
needs a
brand
identity that
communicate
s in a
consistent
manner
across all
touchpoints.

Chapter two

2 Theoretical foundation

The theoretical framework required for creating and executing a brand will be presented in this part.

2.1 Brand

A brand may be thought of as a belief system that was first created to set one's goods apart from those of rival companies.

The early

positioning and branding pioneers were well known. They were familiar with religious practice and knew that a person's conduct might be influenced by their beliefs once they were established. Branding nowadays may be seen as the whole of consumer experiences, made up of visual, tonal, and behavioral brand elements. Understanding a brand's underlying purpose is essential to creating one that resonates with its target market. Color, logotype, and typography are just a few examples of the visual elements that make up a brand. If the brand does not have a clear grasp of where it is headed or what it wants to accomplish, visual elements do not matter as much. Strategy and identity are the two components that make up a brand. Internal components and positioning are included in brand strategy; these components form the basis of the brand. Brand identity includes both visual and verbal expressions that influence how the audience perceives the brand. The bulk of the brand is kept within, so the client only interacts with and sees a little portion of it (everything in Fig. 1 above the water surface).

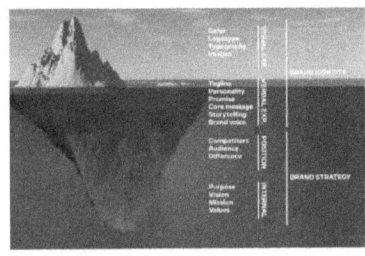

Figure 1: Overview of parts that go into building a brand, based on [10].

Internet start-ups have often been the result of

brilliant ideas rather than placing a lot of emphasis on brand strategy. Brand planning and positioning have often been an afterthought, which has frequently caused issues as the firm has grown. Many businesses today are built on brand, and firms work hard to create brands that their consumers can emotionally relate to. While the word "brand" has a wide range of applications, the most crucial thing is to provide certain fundamental specifications : the name of the firm, its identity (such as its logo or other trademarks), and its goal, vision, values, and positioning. Since doing so would result in a loss of awareness, brand equity, and implementation costs, these fundamental ideas are seldom modified in a brand. Every organization that provides services to clients and operates under a recognized name has a brand. A brand, however, is more than just an iconic logo, a catchy catchphrase, or effective marketing; it speaks for what the firm stands for and is thus crucial for success. Delivering on a promise made to consumers is what a brand is all about. A more complete understanding of a brand is that it expresses authenticity, quality, relevance, and distinctiveness while giving audiences and consumers a unique experience. All of the actions involved in adding value and attracting consumers have a brand as their DNA. Sometimes, businesses that have been successful in forging a deep emotional connection with their consumers are referred to be "beloved brands."

2.2 Marketing

Branding and a brand are two distinct concepts. Branding

elevates concepts from brand in order to highlight who is giving the value, while brand may be thought of as a promise and core message of what the firm stands for and gives to consumers. Too frequently, brand and branding are confused, but just employing brand's graphics may not always address the brand's primary message or experience.

2.2.1 Human psychology

The ideals and emotions that receivers and consumers are moved by influence how a brand develops and evolves. It's critical to comprehend some of the fundamental psychological principles underlying the human mind in order to develop a brand that buyers can relate to. The ego, the id, and the superego are Sigmund Freud's hypothesized divisions of the mind. According to Freud, the id may be located in the subconscious, governs desire principles, and is in charge of our biological impulses. People's environments, which include societal laws, regulations, and views that we pick up from our surrounds, work together to form the superego. Freud described the ego as the intermediary and decision-mak er between the more lust-driven unconscious id and the environmentally regulated superego. In his book Think Fast and Slow, Nobel laureate Daniel Kahneman categorizes the many components of the human mind. Instead of three sections, Kahneman prefers to split the system into two: the slow, energy-intens ive system 1, which is in charge of making judgments based on reasons and consideration s, and the faster, impulse-drive n system 2, which makes decisions based on intuition. Both models are abstractions of a highly complicated system assembly, and it is difficult to pinpoint which system is in use at any one moment. Yet, other studies reveal that up to 80% of consumer choices are made using the quick-thinking system, or system 1 (or the "id," as Freud referred to it). The senses of sight, hearing, smell, taste, and other sensory impressions are used to trigger consumer perception in different ways. The client conceptualizes stimuli that elicit an emotional response and are powerful enough to overcome perception. Unconscious conceptualiza tion serves as the foundation for the customer's first assessment and subsequent recognition.

2.3 Brand encounter

Companies search for novel approaches to emotionally connect with consumers, stand out from competing brands, and establish enduring connections. Value is assessed based on the experiences that consumers have. Instead than relying only on marketing to persuade customers to purchase their goods or services, consumers are continually asking, "Does my experience as a buyer line up with the expectation established by the brand?" It's critical to initially construct the outer layers that the client will interact with in order to produce Usability and a user experience (UX) that they are happy with (see fig 2). These layers are made up of Desirability and Brand experience. The typical visitor will only remain on a website for 10 to 20 seconds, according to Nielsen Norman Group, unless the business explicitly expresses its value proposition and offers a desired desirability.

Figure 2 shows the components that make up a brand, ranging from usefulness to brand experience.

2.3.1 Brand experience: What is it?
The views a person has of a brand

before, during, or after engaging with it or being exposed to it are referred to as their brand experience. Our regular interactions with businesses and the experiences they provide us leave a lasting impression. A person's perception of a brand may be influenced in a variety of active and passive ways, such as by direct and purposeful actions like visiting the business website or contacting customer service (commonly referred to as the customer experience). The visual identity and communication nevertheless influence

people's
perceptions
and form a
part of the
brand
experience
even when
they do not
directly
contact with
the brand.
Clients often
hear this
quote from
the branding
consultancy
Saffron:
"Brand is the
promise of an
experience -
fulfilled." An
expensive
degree of
brand

experience is not required. The fact that it is consistent and in line with the company's brand concept and key message is its most crucial feature.

2.3.2 From what place did brand experience come?

We're in the Golden Era of Branding

right now.
There are
more options
than ever for
companies to
find their
market niche
and establish
direct contact
with their
clients and
supporters.
But, the
history of
branding
truly dates
back
hundreds of
years.
Throughout
time, this
subject and
art form have
developed

into a crucial component of creating any successful organization.

Illustration by Vladanland

While branding truly dates back to the 1500s, there were significant changes in the 19th and 20th centuries. Over years of trial and error and technological development, businesses have figured out how to stand out from the competition, grab consumers' attention, and convert apathetic customers into brand devotees. Finding out this intriguing past is an essential step in creating your own brand.

Background of branding

Beginnings of branding in the 1500s Industrial Revolution from the 1750s to the 1870s. 1870s to 1920s: The innovation period

1920s to 1950s: Branding on the radio

1950s through 1960s: The advent of contemporary branding

1961 to 1990: Branding matures

2000s – Present: Extraordinary branding

Beginnings of branding in the 1500s

The term "brandr" means "to

burn" in the Scandinavian language of Ancient Norse. A brand was first characterized as a burning piece of wood and subsequently as a torch. Cattle were often branded to indicate ownership by the 1500s.

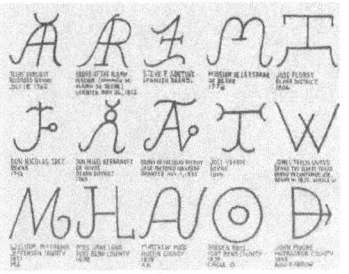

A diagram of
ancient cattle
brands via
Texas State
Historical
Association

Making your
mark—both
practically
and
metaphoricall
y—was at the
heart of
branding
from the
beginning.
Every

branding mark was particular to the cow ranch. The tried-and-true cornerstones of every successful brand, they were straightforward, unique, and immediately recognisable. Imagine these symbols as the first brand logos.

2.3.3 Brand experience design

Always start with the brand concept while creating a brand experience.
An iterative approach that involves designing and testing is used to create brand experiences.
It is not feasible to compete for consumers by imitating other

businesses over the long run.

Determining the most important value that consumers place on a product or service, then putting all of your efforts towards maximizing that value exchange, is a more successful strategy.

There are many stages that make up the process of

developing a brand experience:

• Specify the message - The brand concept, which may be thought of as the company's core, is the message that the business want to convey. People (internal and external) may connect to the firm because of its brand concept, which gives it authenticity. The company's brand strategy has to provide a clear statement about the brand concept, which should be created after studying the target market. Define the terms "visual, linguistic, and behavioral assets"

Design is the ideal medium for conveying the brand's concept and message to the public. A holistic design approach must be used when creating products, settings, systems, and behavior. The following components must cooperate to provide a cohesive message. As well as motion—the manner that animations move, microinteractions, and other transitions of moving content—visual identity also includes components like the brand logo, typography, iconography, photography, and drawings. Voice tone: If used properly, a brand's voice tone can be quite potent and provide a lot of value to a business. The character that the organization established in previous brand planning phases serves as the foundation for the tone of voice. Visual elements and communication style may be significantly impacted by voice tone. Conduct and attitude - A company's behavior is determined by its values and brand personality. It dictates how staff members should conduct themselves in order to "live" the brand and how all customers, regardless of status, should engage with

corporate
workers.

- Clearly
define
contact
points   -
Businesses
and
organizations
need to know
which   touch
points   best
meet   their
requirements
. To create a
seamless
experience,
all
touchpoints—
whether they
are active or
passive, like
advertising or
user

interfaces—must collaborate.

• Moments of truth - A "moment of truth" is only a time when the brand needs to fulfill the promise it has made. Companies must thus consider the expectations of their consumers and ensure that they are satisfied in every circumstance.

Regardless of how positive other past encounters have been, one negative experience at a particular touch-point can negatively affect the customer's overall image of the brand.

• Disrupt via experience – It's crucial to continuously question accepted standards and give user experience first priority if you want to build a brand that endures and stands out. Look beyond the box - Companies may provide distinctive experiences to their consumers by examining the preconceived notions they have about comparable services and goods. Designing an experience that defies convention and assumptions by placing a stronger emphasis on the user and the consumer is preferable to doing so. The brand can create a complete experience by stimulating all the senses. Brands are significantly more likely to become disruptive if they concentrate on the emotion they want their consumers to experience.

2.4 Corporate identity

If a brand concept is not complemented by excellent design, it will not communicate or engage as effectively. Both internally and publicly, the appropriate design can support brand messaging. It is clear from looking at some of the most well-known digital firms of today that they gave design little thought when they were first getting started. Very often, the only thing they had was a logo, or at most, a wordmark. Just a small percentage of them put any effort into creating a visual identity that was based on a clear brand strategy. If the technology, service, or product offered is sufficiently revolutionary , this may work for a time. Nevertheless, when a firm expands and begins to communicate across several touchpoints, the need for a solid visual identity system becomes essential. As a result, many of today's IT behemoths have altered their strategies and begun placing a greater emphasis on the design component.

2.4.1 Definition of brand identity

Humans are visual creatures, and although hearing and smell come into play early on, sight is still the main way we interact with the environment. We seldom ever consume anything without first giving it a closer look, even if it smells delicious. If we hear a sound, we utilize our eyes to determine where it is coming from and what it means. The visual features of a brand are significant, but a method for defining a company's identity must also take into account the experience that gives the brand life.

Brand personality 2.4.2

Certain
brands are
successful in
forging a
stronger
bond with
their
audience,
despite the
fact that all
brands are
businesses
built to
engage in
transactional
relationships
with
customers. A
lot of
businesses
that connect
with their
consumers on
this level are

constructed with a strong connection to archetypes.

2.4.3 Brand slogan

A brand concept is quite unlike from a brand slogan. Although the brand slogan is meant to convey a message to the public, the brand concept encapsulates all your firm stands for. A tagline ought to be honest, engaging, and memorable. Nike's slogan, "Just Do It," is among the most well-known instances of a tagline. It captures the essence of Nike's brand and conveys the concept that everyone can be an athlete. A tagline may engage with consumers via a variety of communicati on strategies.

- Descriptive - Describes the promise made by a product or service to the consumer, as the juice business Innocent's "Nothing but nothing but fruit."
- Superlative - Is employed to establish oneself as the best in a market category, like in the case of

the automobile manufacturer BMW's slogan, "The ultimate driving machine."

• Imperative - Often used to convey the direction of the business or to compel customers to take action. Nike's slogan, "Just do it," serves as one illustration.

• Provocative - Makes the customer think by often

using a question that is both provocative and ironic. Take the phrase "Think tiny" from the VW automaker.

• Particular - Emphasizes the company's product or service, as DuPont's "Better goods for better life via chemistry"

2.4.4 creating a brand's identity

More than simply a logo, color scheme, and font, design is a toolbox that influences a brand's visual behavior across all of the company's contact points. Motion principles, color schemes, typefaces, UX (user experience), and UI are only a few of the guidelines, components, and behaviors that make up brand design (user interface). Together, these values shape how clients see and engage with the company. Design is both a noun and a verb; it is a term for describing, conceiving,

planning, and implementing an idea as well as the concept, artifact, and result of a process.
Two stages may be used to separate the design process [11]:

First step: laying the groundwork
The exploration step entails identifying the visual areas that link and fit

with the company's positioning the best. deciding which typefaces, colors, motion references, materials, and forms best reflect the attitude and personality of the brand.

- Design phase: Based on visual regions, design ideas are established.

Design components are evaluated on the company's touchpoints and primary applications.
• During the development phase, there is an evaluation phase when all design elements and tests are reviewed. Based on this phase's findings, a design system is formed that

governs the future "feeling" and essence of the brand. The framework may be applied to services, goods, symbols, and the whole experience and is intended to be used as a reference. Instead of being a collection of guidelines that must be followed, the design

system is
intended to
serve as a
guiding
document
that reflects
the sentiment
and concept
of the brand.
In order to
preserve
consistency
in the eyes of
the customer,
it is
preferable
not to change
certain
features
(such as the
brand name),
but just
offering a
design

system based on rules and regulations can, over time, result in personnel working with design becoming ignorant.

- Rollout phase - At this time, everything is implemented and more individuals are engaged in interpreting the design ideas. All of the company's contact points are used to test the implemented document, and improvements are made as necessary.

Step 2: Specifying your needs
An knowledge of the brand's four vectors, from communications and product design to environment

and behavior, is necessary to develop this strategy and make it visible for workers to apply across the many touch-points of the company. It will be simpler to simplify the identity to include just the most important components once the brand strategy is better and more clearly understood. For instance, a business that is primarily focused on communications must center their brand identity on functions and duties that are unique to them. The emphasis should be on tone of voice, typography, imagery, and attitude when it comes to communicati on-driven companies (offline or online). Designing brand strategy in such a manner that internal interpreters may apply it with their own creative freedom can help maintain communication current and engaging.

2.5 Branding tactics
While a contemporar

y firm is made up of several moving elements, from the customer's point of view, they only see the various aspects of a single product. There is just one interface that links people to the company from their point of view. The interface is the channel via which value flows and is offered to the client. It includes services, advertisements, websites, and interactions with staff members. Prior to beginning the creative process of developing the brand's graphics, it is crucial to do research and comprehend the audience's makeup and

requirements
.

2.5.1 Brand strategy: what is it?

A company's brand strategy describes what it does, how it does it, and why it does it. These inquiries must have a thorough, understandable response that is comprehensive. According to research, motivated workers are three times more productive than unmotivated ones. Individuals spend nearly a third of their lives at work, which makes it necessary for businesses and organizations to inspire and encourage workers. It becomes essential to have a defined brand strategy that aligns with the values of the personnel. The following stages are involved in defining a brand strategy: Ask, hear, reflect, and adjust.

• Inquire - Employees and management of the firm must inquire as to why the organization exists, beyond financial considerations, as well as to discover strengths and what sets them apart from other businesses, in order to determine the company's driving force.

• Listen - Pay attention to what clients are saying about the business. Ask them what makes your brand unique compared to other businesses that compete in the same market. The goal is to identify or create a differentiator that you can own.

• Consider - Identify significant findings and consider how to express them based on the data gathered in earlier phases. Create them as inspirational and instructive messages for consumers and staff. Create succinct, concise statements that capture the spirit of the brand.

• Refine – The last step involves testing the brand concept that has been developed to see whether it is applicable to external audiences, demonstrates value to them, will be comprehended, and is distinctive enough to set itself apart from rivals. Does it inspire workers, and is it a cause they can support? It is crucial to make sure that everyone in the company follows the brand's communicati on after the brand strategy has been defined. Businesses that fail to live true to their established brand principles often run into issues along the road.

Touch-points , 2.5.2 Figure 6 illustrates the many touch-points that make up a brand. Every touchpoint offers a chance to raise awareness and foster a sense of loyalty among customers.

Figure 6 illustrates the many touchpoints for branding.

Making every touchpoint as efficient and "on brand" as feasible is the goal of effective design. There are numerous touchpoints to take into account, and there is a growing need to make it easy for consumers to travel between them. For businesses, it is now a challenging process to translate information, insight, and purpose into each of these touchpoints. These touchpoints should be seen by businesses as a chance to improve client engagement. Every of a company's touchpoints must integrate UX. Whether it is in sales, customer service, or smartphone engagement, the UX philosophy must be used. Choosing which brand features to apply and deploy on certain contact points is crucial for ensuring that the brand identity is consistent and comprehensive. A contemporary digitally native brand must have a simple structure that includes a symbol for the app icon, typography, colors, motion, tone of voice, and UX principles. To provide consumers with a seamless experience, the fundamental touch-point categories of product, behaviors, environment, and systems must be woven together.

2.5.3 Business Rivals

A thorough awareness of competitors is necessary to position a new brand in a cutthroat market. Brand analysis is a technique for assessing and contrasting the positions that various brands have taken. This strategy involves asking a lot of questions about your rivals, including who they are, who they target as customers, how they position themselves, how they speak to customers, what their USP is, and so on. The process of determining the place the brand will attempt to occupy in customer perception is known as market sector analysis.

• Economics - Sales price is often a factor in the success of companies that are positioned within the category. often promoted as offering more value for less money.

• Mid-market - Created and priced for

middle-class consumers. gives the impression of being of a better caliber and standard than economy, while maintaining value for the money.

• Premium - Intended for middle- and upper-class consumers. Focused on luxury, often preying on customer needs and expectations.

Under these categories, visual language is employed in various ways to elicit certain responses or feelings from customers. Economical companies often use straightforward design, muted color schemes, and plain images. Mid-market companies may employ a wide variety of colors and fonts and are more ornamental. Luxury and high-end companies return to simplicity. The time and care with which brands develop their brand look is what distinguishes economic brands from luxury ones. In addition to carefully selecting their colors and typefaces, premium businesses make a great effort to tell their brand narrative and provide consumers with an engaging experience. By heightening the sense of luxury and the narrative of a "exotic lifestyle," premium businesses draw in new consumers and retain those they already have.

2.5.4 Goals and objectives

Mission and vision statements are often confused. The mission statement outlines the company's goals, objectives, and strategy for achieving them, while the vision statement outlines the company's position in the future. Typical inquiries used to determine a company's vision and goal include: Vision

• What are our aspirations and hopes? What issue are we resolving for overall good? Who and what are we encouraging to change, and why? Mission

What should
we do?
What and
how do we
serve those
we serve?
2.5.5
Clientele
Personas
have been
included into
business
design
processes to
better
understand
their
customers
ever since
Cooper first
introduced
them in 1999.
Personas are
a "fictitious,"

detailed, and tangible portrayal of the target audience. A persona represents target consumers who all have similar demands and behavioral traits. By using personas, designers may narrow their attention to a single person or small group of people, moving away from the goal of designing for everyone. A detailed persona description should contain information about the person's age, gender, habits, profession, needs, worries, and ambitions..

Chapter three

3 Techniques

The research methodologies employed for the study are described in this section.

3.1 A diamond in two

A design sprint or creative process may be visualized using the double diamond design model. The procedure is divided into four steps (see fig. 7):

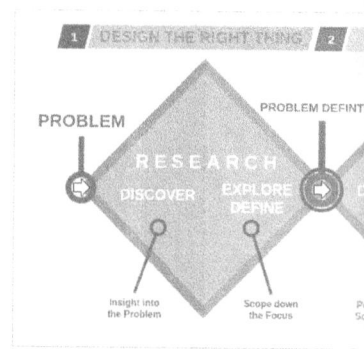

Figure 7: A picture illustrating the creation of a double diamond.

- Discover – At this stage, the issue

domain is researched. The discovery phase begins broadly and entails looking into and comprehending the problem's background. Research, stakeholder interviews, and other workshop activities may all be used to identify and articulate the issue.

- Define – In phase two,

the fundamental issue is identified. This phase entails sifting the information obtained during the discovery phase and focusing on the specific issue at hand. This is a crucial moment to consider if the original issue is still relevant or whether earlier research has altered our understanding of the issue.

• Develop - The investigation and testing of potential solutions to the issue is the development phase. By making low quality prototypes or mock-ups that can be tested on the target audience, you may learn more about potential solutions and gain feedback on them.

• Deliver - The last step is to provide the ultimate answer to the issue.

analyzing the lessons acquired from the earlier stages of development and selecting a single solution that can be tested on consumers. If the results are not as anticipated, it is acceptable to repeat the design process.

Interviews (3.2)
To elicit knowledge and understanding from participants, semi-structured interviews are employed. Interviews that are semi-structured enable the interviewer to

deviate from the predetermined list of questions and let the discussion go in any direction. To elicit additional information on a topic, you may add new questions such, "Can you tell me more about that...?" or "How does what you just stated connect to...?"

Chapter four

4 Method
The techniques utilized to develop a brand identity and strategy for the startup firm are described in this section. The fit of the double diamond design

method with the brand development process led to its selection. To learn more about and have a better grasp of the process of establishing a brand, a literature review and interviews with professionals in the industry were done. A branding workshop with 11 exercises was created and implemented with the company's founders based on data acquired through literature research and interviews. The workshop and literature review's information was utilized to develop a new brand identity for the business website. The target market for the business was then used to assess the website's appeal in order to gauge its effectiveness.

4.1 Review of the literature

To learn more about the branding process, current frameworks, and best practices, a literature research was done. The study investigated the components of a brand as well as how visual aspects like color, typography, and logotype are employed to support brand positioning and messaging. The review's primary objective was to respond to the research questions posed in section 1.2.

Interviews
(4.2)
A series of
semi-structur
ed interviews
(see section
3.2) was
conducted
with five
specially
chosen
branding
industry
professionals.
These
interviews
were
conducted to
learn more
about the
ideal
strategies,
typical
mistakes, and

general brand-buildi ng procedure. LinkedIn was used to get in touch with the interview subjects. Via an online video conference, 30 to 45 minutes were spent individually interviewing each member. The discussions were taped so that any discoveries could be analyzed

afterwards.
Before the
interviews,
seven
open-ended
questions
related to the
study topics
(see section
1.2) were
created.
Appendix B
contains a
brief
summary of
each
interviewee
and the
queries used.

Workshop
4.3
The
company's

founders participated in a workshop on brand creation. The training began with a verbal introduction to brand and all of its components that lasted for ten minutes. There were 11 exercises in the program, and each one began with an introduction. The session, which took three days and a total of 21 hours to complete, was conducted with the two firm founders. The collaborative whiteboard platform Miro 1 and the video communication technology Zoom 2 were used to conduct the session online. A general description of each workshop activity's content is provided below (see appendix C for all workshop questions). The activities of the workshop were carried out in the

the following list:
1. Brand purpose - The first activity included figuring out the company's

purpose, which goes beyond its business goals. By addressing the why and to whom the firm wants to give value questions, the mission of the company may be identified.

2. Vision mission - The previously determined brand purpose serves as the foundation for the

company's
vision and
mission.

3. Core values
- Defines the
company's
core values
by coming up
with core
value
statements
using a
variety of key
terms.

4. Audience
persona -
Creates a
fictitious
character
based on
research into
the
company's
target

market. The procedure entails creating a psychographic and demographic segmentation of the persona as well as emotional and personality insights.

5. A competitor audit looks at how the company may set itself apart from rivals by analyzing

their brand identities, personalities, designs, and user experiences. The competitor audit exercise was carried out on an Excel spreadsheet 3 with distinct tabs for each of the examined firms.

6. USP - Develops the business's USP (unique selling proposition).

identifies potential differentiators by reviewing the content of rival audits.

7. Brand positioning - Sets the brand positioning of the business. Target audience, pain points, major benefits, rivals, and differentiators are the five categories that this exercise

divided the information from each of the previous ones into.

8. Brand personality - Based on the target market and rivals, a brand personality and archetype are developed. The tone of voice a brand chooses to connect with its audience depends on its personality.

9.   The brand's core message is developed. This is the message that the brand intends to communicate to the public. This message is made by adding one of the following questions to the several categories established in the sixth exercise: who, what, why, how, where, or when.

10. Storytelling - Develops a structure for the consumer's relationship with the brand. provides insight into the information and message that should be sent at each individual contact point.

11. Brand tagline - The last task involves creating a

brand slogan by generating ideas for phrases using various keywords.

4.4 Test and prototype
Based on inputs from a brand creation workshop, the corporate website's design, brand color, and logotype were created (see section 4.3). Testing and design were

done in iterations.

4.4.1 Research on the target audience

Using social media, 13 friends of the researcher who were identified as belonging to the target demographic (described in 4.3, exercise 4) were invited to offer their opinions on the brands and websites they found attractive. 22 websites and companies were gathered, investigated, and contrasted for similarity (see fig 8).

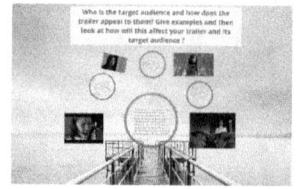

Screenshots of websites that individuals in the target demographic visited are shown in Figure 8.

9 Strategies for Reaching Your Target Audience

Follow your emotions. Going with your emotions is the only effective approach to connect with anybody or any group of people. Incorporate time, communicate your brand's values, collaborate with

influencers, provide case studies, and work with them.
Never Stop Developing Your Brand's Image; Quit Sounding Pushy; Pose inquiries

Brand Desirability (4.4)
We refer to brand attractiveness as the degree to which a given client segment finds

a particular brand to be appealing and desired. It occurs when there is a strong value fit, or when customer values are strongly aligned with those of the brand.

A brand will be able to keep consumers for the long run and convert them into fans if it can successfully deliver on its promise across as many brand touchpoints as feasible. Throughout the course of many businesses' brand growth, brand attractiveness increases; this is a process that requires perseverance and patience.

After a strong brand's

desirability has been attained, brand management must work to keep it there via strategic action.

Which hues best reflect the company? A brand's colors are a collection of five to ten shades that are used to represent a certain company. By applying brand colors consistently and intelligently, brand awareness and recognizabilit y may be increased. The team may evaluate design concepts and ideas by using low fidelity (lo-fi) designs, which are the initial iteration of a future product. The quickness of innovation and simplicity of design are two crucial qualities of low fidelity.

A mid-fidelity prototype is one that is more realistic and comprehensive. Some design elements or interactions are often tested with it. To evaluate the user experience and get feedback on the overall design, a high-fidelity prototype that as nearly resembles the final product as possible is employed. An individual typeface that forms a distinctive aspect of your visual brand identity is known as a brand font. These will be included in the standards for your brand, which will make it easier for you to maintain consistency when producing new materials like business cards, sell sheets, pamphlets, billboards, social media visuals, and more.

Chapter five

5 Discussion

The following is how the research questions posed in section 1.2 have been addressed.
What elements make up a brand?
The subject of what constitutes a brand's constituent parts is addressed through the literature

research and conducted interviews.

Fig. 1 depicts the different components of the procedure.

The literature study and the interviews provided a strong platform on which more work could be carried out.

How can a start-up business build a brand that resonates

with its audience?

One strategy that may be used to develop and build a brand that resonates with its target audience is suggested by the created workshop activities carried out in section 4.3. All of the company's founders acknowledged the value of the workshop activities and said they had improved their understanding of the significance of positioning and branding. It became evident that everyone in the workshop needed to be knowledgeable with the brand and have a "decision-making position" inside the organization since these choices set the foundation for how the brand talks, looks, and acts. Having workers participate in this workshop without having a "decision-ma king role" would probably result in uneven design language or other types of inquiry over time. Just a little amount of scholarly literature has been written on the usage of archetypes in brand building. The usage of archetypes, however, made it simpler to define and construct how the brand should be seen. This served as the building blocks for the words used to characterize the brand in the subsequently carried out attractiveness test. How can consumers be used to test a new brand? The findings suggest that the Microsoft desirability test may be used to examine and gauge how the public thinks and perceives a recently launched brand. The data shows that the brand's desired "feelings" and how the target audience interacted with them on the corporate website are consistent. The top five emotions among the target population were selected for each of the five words used to describe the brand. The idea that the brand is tailored to the intended target group is strengthened by the fact that respondents who were not in the target group used different terms to describe the product. The fact that the test's word order was randomly determined for each participant lessens the influence of "lazy responders," who would only choose the first five words from the list, on the findings.

The selection of words for the exam, however, is a factor that should be taken into account. Words may signify various things to different people. I was able to choose which terms to use and which to modify by conducting an initial test in which some participants were questioned on their interpretations of the words.

5.1 Conclusion

The three goals of this study were to first create a framework

that
businesses
could use to
create their
own brands,
then use that
framework to
create and
design a
brand for a
company
operating in a
particular
industry, and
finally
implement
the newly
developed
brand on the
company
website and
evaluate its
effect on the
audience that

the company
is trying to
reach. A
company's
chances of
succeeding in
the
marketplace
may be
increased by
having a well
considered
brand
strategy and
identity,
according to
a study of the
literature and
expert
interviews.